Sage & Smudge

Secrets of Clearing Your Personal Space

by Donna Stellhorn

Requests and inquiries may be mailed to:
ETC Publishing House
Reno, Nevada
www.etcpublishing.com

First Edition, First Printing 1999
Second Printing 2000
Third Printing 2001
Fourth Printing 2002
Fifth Printing 2003
Sixth Printing 2004
Seventh Printing 2005

ISBN 0-9641339-5-4

Concepts presented in this book derive from traditional
European and American metaphysical and folk lore. They
are not to be understood as directions, recommendations
or prescriptions of any kind. Nor does the author or
publisher make any claim to do more than provide
information and report this lore.

Table of Contents

Sage and Smudging

The sage stick she held in her hand flamed as she lit it and then began to smolder. The stick was about 6 inches long and an inch in diameter wrapped together with colorful thread. The sage twigs glowed and the smoke rose in a dance, as smoke does. The strong herb smell mingled with the air in the room and a sense of peace spread through each of us. She moved gracefully towards the door; then guided the stick around the contours of the door, watching the smoke rise towards the ceiling.

Then she moved to a chair and slowly moved the smoldering stick of sage around it. Sometimes the smoke rose upward, sometimes it moved sideways, and she watched and noted how it moved. She lingered where the smoke pattern didn't please her. She moved from object to window, from window to door, not missing any piece of furniture or place of importance. She did this throughout the room and then throughout the house. Finally she crushed out the burning end of the stick on the porch and pronounced the house cleansed. This is smudging.

History

Smudging, or burning sage in a ritual manner is a Native American tradition for healing, clearing a space and as a religious ceremony. The original meaning of the ritual was that the rising smoke carried the request to Spirit. In modern times Sage is often used to remove household odors, and is said to alleviate airborne germs. Native Americans burned sage to clear both the mind as well as the home.

Sage has long been considered a 'cure-all'. In Latin it's name, "Salvia", means 'to be saved'. In the 17th Century, John Evelyn wrote "… a plant indeed with so many wonderful properties…it is said to render men immortal." However, when that was not possible, Sage was planted near the graves in England to ensure the death would bring salvation in heaven.

In Roman times, Sage was used in the baths to soothe aching muscles and tired feet. In the Middle Ages, Sage was a very popular medicine and was used to cure everything from coughing to venereal disease. Sage was used to dye hair black. It was also often eaten as a fritter, the leaves fried in batter and sprinkled with lemon juice and served at the end of the meal to help digestion. In China, Sage tea is a popular beverage for quieting the nerves and keeping one well.

Folklore says if you want a wish to come true, you write it on a sage leaf and sleep with it under your pillow. It has also been said that wise people always kept it in their garden, and if the master of the house was ill, the sage would wilt.

Sage is considered a "hot herb", and therefore provides energy when burned. It is ruled by the planet Jupiter, the planet of expansion. We experience this expansion as the smoke moves through the air. Some see Sage as bringing wisdom, others note a connection spiritually.

Types of Sage

All counted, there are more than 500 species of Sage grown today. There are two types of Sage commonly used for smudging. One is *Salvia Officinalis L.*, the Latin name of our common garden and wild sage, a member of the mint family. Most varieties of Sage come from this branch of the mint family. Originally from southern Europe, sage has been found in the United States since the time of the European settlers. The other type of Sage we see, common in smudge sticks, is actually not related to the culinary Sage and is called "Sagebrush". Both types are considered acceptable for smudging purposes.

Sage is a perennial with one of the more familiar varieties having wooly-white/grey leaves and growing up to 2 feet high. Smudge sticks made from this white sage are usually small, about 2-3 inches in length. The other, wild sage, is more of a twig with small leaves and sometimes violet-blue flowers. This sage, found in the mountains of the west, is made into larger sticks—often tied tightly with colorful string or thread.

White Sage

White Sage has long been a culinary herb, used in soups and stuffings, and has a warm and slightly bitter taste. When burned it smells somewhat like a mix of sweet cannabis and camphor. The wild Sage is generally not used in cooking but can be burned as smudge. It may smell slightly less sweet than the white sage, but is otherwise very similar.

Making a Smudge Stick

Gather Sage in June and July for drying. Be careful with the leaves as they are delicate,and whole leaves are needed for making smudge sticks. If only loose sage is desired than smaller leaves are fine. Gather Sage after the dew has dried. Cut branches, leaving enough stem to tie with string—maybe an inch or two. Cut only a few branches from each plant, so as not to damage the plant permanently. Some people like to leave an offering to the plant when they take a part of it. A wonderful offering would be to water the plant, thanking it for its gift to you and the world.

To make a smudge stick you will need a small handful of Sage leaves and twigs, and some string or embroidery floss (available at craft and fabric stores) in a color you like, such as red or blue. The sage does not have to be completely dried to make the smudge stick, in fact, if it is still a bit moist it is easier to tie the sticks together.

Smudge Stick

Sage needs to be completely dried before being burned. This drying process can take from a month to a year depending on conditions. Dry this herb in a cool, dark, well ventilated place. After tying the stalks together lay them on a screen or drying rack. If drying on a rack, turn weekly until dry.

On a full moon take the sage and gather it so all the stems face the same direction. Wrap a string around the base of the stems nine times, being careful to leave loose ends of two or three inches. Continue wrapping the string around the rest of the sage and back down again crossing the string nine times. Finally, wrap the base again nine times. Tie the end to the original loose end tightly and cut off the tails of the string. If the sage needs additional drying then hang the stick up in the kitchen for a week or so.

Smudge sticks can also be made with ingredients in addition to the Sage. You can have Juniper surrounded by sage in your stick or mingle the sage with lavender. Either would have a cleansing effect as you smudge.

Loose Sage

Sage leaves do not have to be bundled into a stick to be used for smudging. Many of us urban gardeners collect rather small leaves from our Sage plants—plants that are not large enough to be a stick yet. The Sage can be used in the loose-leaf form. Dry the sage

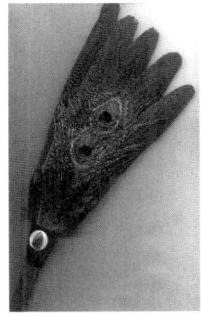

Smudge Fan

on wire racks or paper towels, turning them every couple of days. When the Sage leaves are completely dry, the Sage can be stored in a glass jar for future use.

Shells and Fans

Just as the smoke in the smudging process is our message, the Smudge Fan is our messenger. A Smudge Fan can be as simple as a single feather, or as complex as an ornately decorated wing of feathers.

In some traditions, loose Sage is burned in a Shell, usually abalone, and the smoke is wafted through the room or space by waving a Smudge Fan over the smoldering Sage. The

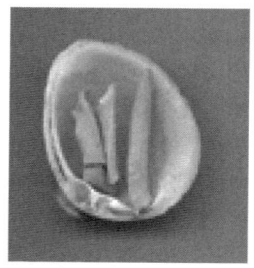

Smudge Shell

Shell is cupped in the palm of the hand or balanced on the tips of fingers as the bottom of the shell can get quite hot. The smoke that rises is almost patted or encouraged to move forward, up out and around, in very short, quick motions, using the Fan. While this is done, the Smudger can chant or speak the "clearing" ceremony words. Words could be sung in a Native American dialect or words can be spoken in whatever language you choose. For example, "I ask this house be cleared" or "I demand negativity leave this dwelling" would both be appropriate words for clearing a house.

Loose sage can also be burnt in clay pots, clay dishes or cauldrons. Place a trivet under anything made of clay as the bottom will get very hot. The smoking Sage can be set in the center of the room or on an altar. Objects can then be passed through the smoke to clear and cleanse them.

How to Smudge a Room

To Smudge a room involves walking around the room with the smoldering Sage, so at times it is easier to use a Smudge stick rather than the loose Sage. Always smudge with care. If a breeze from a fan or open window catches loose burning Sage leaves, they may be spread around the room, perhaps causing something else to catch fire. When you smudge a room the smudge stick may drop some burning ash, so you may want to carry a dish with a little water in it to catch the ash before it hits your good Oriental rug.

Apply flame to the Sage stick until the smoke rises clearly, then wait until the flame dies down so it smolders, do not shake out the flame but let it subside naturally. Carry the stick in your power hand (the hand you write with) and move to the main door in the room (or, if there is more than one door, choose the one closest to you). Trace around the door in a clockwise motion following the outline of the molding around the door. Then proceed around the room toward your right (clockwise), stopping at each window to trace around it, and each door to do the same. As you approach pieces of furniture, move the stick above them and below them keeping the plate or dish underneath the Smudge stick to catch any ash than might fall on your good furniture.

As you move around the room, you may state aloud that you wish the room cleared of negativity, that you wish peace and joy to enter, and that evil must leave. You can call on help to accomplish this from ancestors, angels, guides or the Universe in general.

As you Smudge, notice how the smoke moves. Pause every few feet and watch the smoke rise. If it rises straight up, the area is clear. But if the smoke seems to turn or move oddly, there may rest some negative energy, a mischievous spirit, or a connection to someone who wishes you ill. Note where in the room this negative energy is and what object it may be connected to. Sometimes we have items in our homes that for some reason have collected some negative energy. They may have been bought used and still have the energy of the previous owner, or maybe they were gifts from people who were not on the best terms with you.

To clear this particular space hold the Smudge stick in place until the smoke rises straight up. If it is around an object, pass the object through the smoke several times, and then hold the smoldering sage stick above the object and see if the smoke will rise straight up.

Continue around the room until you reach the place you started and cross that place to complete the circle. Then extinguish your Smudge stick. Smudge sticks can be saved for future use.

Grinding a Smudge stick out is the preferred method for extinguishing it, but sometimes it is difficult to put out a smudge stick. Indications that your smudge stick may still be burning are that you can still see a smoldering flame inside, or that smoke is still rising from the Smudge stick. An alternative way to extinguish your stick is to put the burning end of the smudge stick into a cup of sand or salt. As a last resort, you can douse the burning end in water although this is considered inappropriate. It is best to extinguish your smudge stick using a compatible element like Earth.

How to Smudge the House

Smudging a house is simply an extension of Smudging a room. As you proceed from room to room, the Smudge stick may not give off as much readable smoke as you move through the house. It is considered acceptable to relight the Smudge stick as you go. Smudge sticks can be lit using a match, lighter, or candle.

When Smudging an entire house you can begin the ceremony at your altar. If you don't have an altar, begin in the Kitchen (the power center of the house). Move through each room as described above and then move to the next room as you would naturally, following the wall to the door and then through the door and so on.

When you come to closets it is perfectly alright to just briefly wave the stick inside the closet, or you might end up with clothes that smell very much like Sage. Bathrooms should be done carefully as they are both wealth and health centers of the house. Garages are optional, if you have an attached garage you can Smudge it as you go through the house.

Move through the house until you return to the room where you started. It is important that you end where you started even though it may mean moving through some rooms twice. Extinguish the stick in the room where you began.

How to Smudge an Object

Objects can be Smudged to clear the energy that may have been picked up either by someone touching that object or by virtue of where the object has been. If you buy a crystal in a store, the crystal most likely has the energy of that store. Smudging brings the energy to a neutral state at which time you can put your own energy into it.

Objects that are usually Smudged are spiritual or ritual items. Tarot cards, Crystals, sacred objects, and statues are all considered spiritual items. It can also be a good idea to smudge objects that are considered normal household items, which you wish to use as 'ritual items'. This might include candles and candle holders, tables, mirrors, utensils, glasses and bowls.

To Smudge an object, pass the object through the smoke several times. Most objects are easily cleared. When you touch the object it will feel like yours, it will feel light and familiar. However, objects received from negative people, or ones you have which remind of old, adversarial relationships may not clear easily, and when you touch the object your thoughts will still turn to that person or situation. In severe cases negative energy enters the house and your life through a mental doorway created by that object. In this case it is better just to remove the item from your home.

How to Smudge a Person

Smudging a person is done for basically two reasons. First it is often done before a person enters a Magical Circle. (This is a circle that is formed for the purpose of gathering energy to cast a spell. See books on Wicca for more information.)

A person may also wish to be Smudged when they come into close contact with someone or something they believe is negative. A person who has witnessed a crime or an act of violence may want to be Smudged. In this vast world we live in, we can sometimes come into contact with people that we just don't feel good about. It can be they are on a very different path than ourselves. People have a right to be on whatever path they choose, and you have the right to not agree with that path, and to cleanse your auric field (the energy field that surrounds you) after contact with them.

To Smudge a person, light the stick and, holding it about 6 inches away from the body, start at the back of their head and wave the stick back and forth as you move slowly down the back of their body. Do not hold the stick over their head. As you move the stick down, they may feel a tingly sensation or a quick shiver. This cleanses the auric field. Move to the front and start smudging about six inches out from the top of the forehead, and move down the body again. Hold each arm out horizontally and move the stick under each arm and out to the finger tips. Then hold the smudge stick behind them once again about midway up their back and still 6 inches away from them. If the smoke rises up they are clear. If it does not, repeat the process a second time.

How to Smudge Yourself

You would smudge yourself for any of the same reasons that you would smudge another person. Light the stick and, keeping it well away from your body, move the stick in small circles in front of you. Begin at your head and move down the front of your body. Extend each arm and move the stick under the arm slowly, letting the smoke rise up and touch your arm. To do your back, move the stick so smoke is rising in front of you and then step through the smoke. Now, by intention, you are clearing the energy behind you. Step through the smoke several times to completely clear your back.

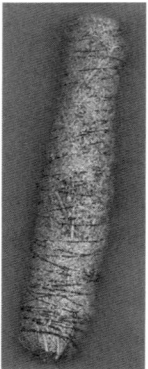

*Flower
Bundle*

Smudging Ceremony

Smudging as part of a ceremony is usually done out of doors. Special Flower Bundles or Sage wreaths are used. The entire bundle is thrown on the fire and each person walks through the smoke. This begins the ceremony. Such ceremonies are outlined in books on Wicca and Shamanism.

When to Smudge

Smudging is the act of clearing and releasing negative energy. So Smudging is best done when the Moon is waning. The Waning Moon is the time between the Full

Moon and the New Moon. As something wanes it becomes less, just as the Moon becomes smaller and smaller.

Smudging can be done in the day or evening. Smudging requires a bit of concentration and observation of how the smoke is moving through the air. It is best done when you will not be disturbed by phone or family members.

It is a good idea to Smudge before you settle into a new home. It is also appropriate to smudge spiritual objects that you bring into your home such as crystals, wands, statues or pictures. You will probably want to smudge when negative people have been in your home and have left some of their energy behind. It can be done when there has been a death or loss connected to your family or friends. (This is not a substitute for grief but part of the ritual of grieving for many cultures.)

Smudging can also be done in the Spring as part of the re-opening of the home to the world. After the Spring cleaning when the windows again are open to the warm breezes, a good house Smudging can clear the energy for new opportunities.

Storing Sage

Sage should be stored in a cool, dry place. Sage should be completely dried if it is to be kept in a closed container. Loose Sage can be stored in a glass jar with a cork top. Smudge sticks can be placed in a drawer or cabinet. Dry Smudge sticks can crumble if knocked about too much, so it is best to keep them out of the way of daily life, yet still accessible when you need them.

Locating Sage and Smudge Sticks

To find Sage for making smudge sticks you can contact natural foods markets where herbs are sold. Also check with local Herbalists. There are a few mail order supply stores that sell herbs in bulk, but be aware a pound of white sage is <u>a lot</u> of white sage! Mail order supply houses usually advertise in Herb and health magazines. You might also consider contacting local Indian reservations to find freshly made smudge sticks.

All Sage and Smudge products
pictured in this book are available from
Moonrise Magic.
Call 1-800-918-2689
or visit the website at
www.moonrisemagic.com

Donna Stellhorn has been an Astrologer for more than 10 years. She currently runs her business, Moonrise Magic, from Boston, Massachusetts. She previously owned and operated Moonrise Books in Albuquerque, New Mexico for more than seven years.

Donna's studies lead to certification as a Master Practitioner in Feng Shui. She also is a practicing Astrologer, certified with both the AFA and Extensions Unlimited. She has written articles and columns for magazines all over the country on various subjects including Astrology, Tarot, Martial Arts, Prosperity, Magical Workings and Feng Shui. She writes a monthly column on Feng Shui for New Mexico's leading Metaphysical Newspaper, "The Light". She is the author of "Fühl Dich wohl mit Feng Shui", published in Switzerland, by Fischer Media. Consultations with Donna are an enlightening and exciting experience.

Donna Stellhorn can be contacted at
moonrise@moonrisemagic.com
or visit our website at
www.moonrisemagic.com

Order Form

Please Fill Out Next Page Also

Items

☐ Mini Smudge Kit with Shell $3.95
☐ Smudge Kit with Shell in clear box $9.95
☐ Blue Sage Smudge Stick $5.95
☐ White Sage Smudge Stick, Large $6.95
☐ White Sage Smudge Stick (mini)
   with Abalone Shell $12.50
☐ Moonrise Magic Catalog .... FREE

Other Books

☐ Candleburning - Secrets of Modern Day Rituals
   for Quick Results $4.95
☐ Color - A Secret Language Revealed $4.95
☐ Tarot - Secrets of Card Reading $7.95
☐ Simple Feng Shui Secrets Book & Mirror Set $11.95
☐ Sage & Smudge - The Ultimate Guide $14.98

Subtotal:_____

Mass. Residents Add 5% State Tax:_____

Shipping (See Chart on Next Page):_____

Total:_____

Order Form

Name ....

Address ....

City, State, Zip ....

Daytime Phone Number ....

Method of payment .... Visa / MC / Disc / Check / MO

Credit Card Number ....

Expiration Date ....

Name On Card ....

Signature ....

Email ....

Copy BOTH Pages of this Order Form
and send it to:
Moonrise Magic
26 Highland Park
Peabody, MA 01960

Email: moonrise@moonrisemagic.com

Or Call 1-800-918-2689

Shipping Charges: Within USA ONLY:
0 - $20 - Add $3.50
$20 - $50 Add $5.00
$50 - $100 Add $7.00
$100 - $200 Add $9.00
Over $200 - Shipping FREE